Life Organization In 1 Month

Take The One Month Self Organization Challenge And Experience The Amazing Benefits

Table of Contents

Introduction

I want to thank you and congratulate you for purchasing this book, *"Organize Your Life In One Month"*. This book contains proven steps and strategies about how to organize your life.

Organizing your life is not a difficult task. This book will help you organize your life by providing you with strategies that promote action. Its main goal is to help you reach your long-term goals. If you have continually failed to reach your goals in the past, then this is the right book for you. By the time you are done with the One-month Challenge, you will be proud of yourself upon seeing that you have accomplished the goals that you set. You will then translate this personal victory to other areas of your life.

Thanks again for purchasing this book, I hope you enjoy it!

Chapter 1 Week 1: Know Yourself

Organizing your life can be a constant battle against laziness. When you fail to do scheduled tasks, you are letting that part of you win. To be successful in this one-month self-organization challenge, it is important that you acknowledge that this part of your personality exists, but that it is not your true self.

Your true self is responsible and can make the right decisions based on the circumstances in front of you. When you are at your best, you can achieve the goals that you put your mind to. However, for you to be at your best, you need to be the person in control of your actions, not the lazy and scared version of yourself.

Though that part of you is not your true self, it is still a significant part of your personality. Most of the time, it is the one taking the reins of your life. That's because most of the time, we make decisions based on our emotions.

Most people think that they are using their critical thinking skills to make decisions. However, the truth is that most of us make decisions based on the underlying fears and pleasures embedded deep within our psyche.

We can observe this in ourselves when we are trying to fight off procrastination and start working. Usually, our mind makes us avoid working and do unproductive stuff like checking our phones or taking long naps. Our mind is designed to pick the path of least resistance.

We think and feel that the things that we do when we procrastinate are pleasurable and the things that we should be doing are not. When our willpower is low, we often can't help but chase the pleasurable things and avoid the ones that are not. However, it is actually the less-pleasurable things that help reach goals. There may not be any pleasure felt while doing it, but the pleasure follows after the task is done. The feeling of relief and sense of accomplishment are the rewards.

However most people want to skip the work and jump straight to the rewards. This happens when we do not have enough motivation or energy. For us to constantly have the will to organize our thoughts and the things around us, we need to constantly refuel these two factors.

Week 1 Activity: Assess your habits

To do this, you need to step back from your daily routine and assess your whole life. This is the first part of the One Month Challenge. In this challenge, your goal is to measure your ability to act on the tasks that you set. To do this, we need to gather information about how we use our time and energy. Aside from this, we should also find out about our mindset when we are performing well according to our plans and when we are deviating from them. Only when we have a full grasp of our mind's activity can we start making changes.

Give power to the real you

Before you can start organizing your life, you first need to organize your mind. Specifically, you want to know what you want to achieve. When you are planning your goals, you are giving power to the more productive part of you.

Your goals

On your first day of the One Month Challenge, you need to establish the goals that you want to achieve. Let's do a little exercise:

Take out a piece of paper and pen and sit back in a comfortable quiet environment. Don't do this on your bed or you might fall asleep. When you are ready, close your eyes and start breathing at a regular pace. There will be some thoughts that will randomly come into your mind. You need to clear your mind of those thoughts.

When you have cleared your mind, try to imagine yourself 20 years from now. Imagine yourself after you have achieved most of your life goals. Where are you? Who are the people around you and what are you doing? Answer these questions out loud with as many details as you can, then write them down.

When you are satisfied with your vision, it is time to start creating your goals. You need to think of the goals that you need to achieve to be able to attain your vision. When they are clear to you, you should start listing them all down. You should never water-down your goals. Don't set goals that are lower than what you really want. If you dreamed that you were in a mansion, then set your goals to have a mansion and not some less impressive type of home.

When you can't think of anything else to add to your list, take a step back and review your goals. Now, rephrase them in the present tense. Instead of saying "I will become the CEO of my own multi-million dollar company", rewrite it to say "I am the CEO of my own multi-million dollar company." If you think that some of the goals you have written are too easy, you could double up by increasing the value of the goal. We could even rephrase our previous example to sound like this; "I am the CEO of three multi-million dollar companies."

After stating your goals in words, you need to arrange them chronologically. Let's say you have these two goals:

"I can speak French."

"I am the best performing car salesman in the county."

These two goals are not related, but you want to achieve both of them. These two goals require different sets of actions. In this case, you need to prioritize one over the other. If you are already in a job and you are already starting to make progress in goal number 2, then you may choose to prioritize that goal chronologically.

The next step is to encode these goals and print them in the largest font size that you can use, while still having them fit on one piece of paper. You should then post copies of this in places where you spend most of your time. When you feel that your mind and your environment are too unorganized for progress, you should read these goals to prevent you from deviating from your plan.

Converting long goals to short-term goals

The goals that we stated above are generally long-term goals. Because you imagined yourself twenty years older in our activity at the beginning of the chapter, then we can conclude that you have a 20-year period to achieve these goals. Our aim is for you to achieve all of them within that period and not miss our deadline.

To become more organized in working towards them, we need to convert long-term goals into multiple short-term goals. You can do this by listing down smaller tasks that you can do in shorter durations that lead to your goals. By doing this, you will have more familiarity with the goal that you are trying to achieve. You will know exactly what it takes to reach it.

Your goal timeline

Goals that take years to accomplish need a visual timeline for you to be able to track how near you are to achieving them and how much more time and effort is required to arrive at the goal.

To create a timeline, you will need to distribute the tasks that lead to a long-term goal across the number of years that you assigned to achieve it. If you have a 5-year goal for example, then you can divide the tasks and distribute them across a five-year period. Place them in a table in chronological order.

Create a schedule that you can be proud of

Everybody has 168 hours in a week. Our ability to reach our goals will depend on our ability to spend these 168 hours efficiently and productively.

As we begin our One-Month challenge, we should create a schedule that will allow us to move closer to our goals. When scheduling tasks on a daily basis, we should use our short-term goals.

We should have a system of prioritizing things to be able to know which tasks to put more time and effort on. A popular way of doing this is by dividing your tasks into four categories:

Important and urgent

Important but not urgent

Unimportant but urgent

Unimportant but not urgent

Some people can easily divide their tasks among these four categories correctly. However, some people put unimportant tasks in the important category and try to reason out why they are important. A teenage boy, for example, may put the task of "playing computer games" in the "important but not urgent category" and tell himself; "I also need time to relax and relieve stress." Though the reason may seem valid, that task actually does not fit the reason. Playing video games also makes you tired just like any other task.

Though many adults do not play video games anymore, most still have the habit of giving priority to the wrong tasks. Some adults watch too much TV while others spend too much time browsing through their social media feeds. We often regret overdoing these things when we know that there are truly important things that we should be doing.

You have to be honest with yourself when categorizing your tasks. If you still continue to put tasks in the wrong categories and justify your actions, then you need help from someone close to you in assigning your tasks. You need someone who can think in a logical way for you without being influenced by the fears and pleasures that are controlling your mind.

The tasks for your goals should be assigned to timeslots on a weekly basis. When making your weekly schedule, you need to assign the Important and Urgent tasks first. They are the tasks that have deadlines and are absolutely necessary for the completion of your goal. It is essential to give enough time to these types of tasks to make sure that they are accomplished in the timeslots assigned to them.

Next, you should assign timeslots to goals that are urgent, but not important. These tasks are lifestyle maintenance tasks that are not directly related to your goals. They have deadlines, but accomplishing them will not necessarily bring you closer to your goals. For instance, paying your utility bills is something that you should do immediately, but it is not necessarily essential to reaching your goals. If possible, you should delegate these tasks to people who are capable of doing them.

You should then schedule your "Important but not urgent tasks." These tasks don't have deadlines, but are essential or at least helpful in reaching your goals. For instance, reading a book about running a specific type of business is an example of an important, but not urgent task if your goal is to open your own business. Because these kinds of tasks do not have deadlines, people often fail to prioritize them when scheduling.

Lastly, you should try to remove all the unimportant and not urgent tasks from your schedule. We often do these activities because they are fun and most of the time, addictive. Taking a break to smoke, for example, is not at all important or urgent. People however, have difficulty stopping the habit because the little cancer sticks are extremely addictive.

Starting on a goal

When you are just starting to work on a long-term goal, you don't have a track record that you can base your actions on. With new goals, you need to start by listing down the steps that you need to take to be able to reach them.

If you have no idea what the necessary steps are, you need to do some research. You should look up for people who have achieved goals that are quite similar to yours. Learn about what they did to get what they wanted. Also, take note of the circumstances that they had that are similar to your current situation. You could then decide on a course of action that you can take that will help you achieve your goals.

Goals in progress

It is also possible that you've already started with some of the goals you listed. If you have an action plan for that goal, then you may need to review that action plan. If not, then you really need to create one.

Creating your Action Plan

Planning is essential to success but, by itself, it cannot help you achieve anything. Planning should be followed by the specific right actions stated in the plan. An action plan should be able to answer these essential questions:

What is the intended outcome?

In an action plan, you need to make your goal statement more specific. For example, if your goal is to start your own business in 5 years, then you need to specify what type of business it is and when your opening day will be. You should also brainstorm the products and services your business will provide and what qualities it has against its competition in the area.

Where are you with your goal?

The second thing that you need to include in your action plan is the progress that you have made to reach that goal. Start listing the tasks that you have done to move you closer to that goal. As you continue to finish more tasks related to a particular goal, you need to add those tasks to a list. By doing this, you maintain 100% awareness of the progress you have made in your goals. Being aware of the things you've done in the past for a goal also increases your emotional commitment towards it.

What's left to be done?

Now that you have a clear idea of the specificities of the goal and the progress already done to achieve it, you also need to list the tasks that need to be done. Follow the instructions in the earlier part of the book to assign them into schedules. The optimal habit in creating schedules is weekly. Creating a weekly schedule allows you to manage each day effectively.

You are like a general with a clear view of the battlefield.

What and who do you need?

Now that you know the specific tasks that you need to do, you should already have an idea of the specific requirements of the tasks. Some tasks require cooperation with other people. Some tasks may also require equipment and materials that you still do not have. You need to schedule these tasks according to the availability of the things that you need. If you have the power to delegate, then you should think of the best people to assign urgent, but not important tasks to.

Are we there yet?

Your action plan should also mention how you will measure goals. Measuring your progress allows you to know if you are done with that goal or not. All your short-term goals should be measurable so that you know when you are done with them and can move on to the next goal in your timeline.

Time tracking

As you organize your life, you will realize that two important factors can contribute to your success: time and action. When you take the right actions over a period of time, you will become organized and ultimately, successful.

Now let us begin with how you spend your time. In this activity, all you have to do is to find a notebook and take note of the things that you do every hour for the next thirty days. To avoid forgetting the task of taking down notes, you first need to schedule when you will do it. The ideal times to do it are before you leave for work in the morning, during your morning break in the office, at lunch break, during your afternoon break, before you leave your office, and before you go to sleep. This means, you need to take notes 6 times a day.

You may ask why you need to do this because you already made a schedule. By doing this task, you are trying to monitor your ability to stick to the schedule you set. It will also answer why your progress is so slow and what you can do to hasten it.

At the end of the third day of doing this habit, you need to take the time to analyze how you spent your time. You could even compare it with the schedule that you set. Were there some tasks that you failed to do? Were there tasks that were too difficult for you? Were there tasks that you avoided? The answers to this questions will expose the barriers preventing your from reaching your goals.

You should assess your progress again at the end of the one month challenge.

Chapter 2 - Identifying And Dealing With Goal Barriers

The steps that you take towards your goal, just like any other journey, will be riddled with challenges and difficulties. The bigger your goal is, the more challenges you will face in your journey.

Many of the challenges will be beyond your control and you just have to work around them. There are also those challenges that only exist in your mind. One example of these challenges is your fear. Fear is the source of most of our bad behaviors.

To be able to deal with fears effectively, you need to understand their primary function. Fear is a survival response to stimuli that may be a threat to us. We base our assumption that something is a threat on our past personal experiences and the things that we observe. In the past, when survival was the only priority, this emotion was important in keeping our ancestors alive. These days however, many of the things we fear are not physical threats to us.

For example, a lot of people fear being in front of a crowd. They manifest classic signs of fear like becoming paralyzed and widening of the pupils when they realize that the attention of a lot of people is on them.

If we closely examine the situation however, most modern activities where we need to face a crowd are not life threatening. In fact, the fear of speaking to a large number of people is mostly based on the lack of experience of doing it. We are afraid of embarrassing ourselves or doing something foolish that may affect our reputation. Even if these possibilities could happen however, they are not really life threatening.

If you want a successful life, then you need to be able to deal with these fears. Many successful people claim that they use the things that they are afraid to do as indicators of the things that they should be doing. For instance, there are times when we are afraid to go to our boss to ask for a raise. If you think you deserve a raise but you are afraid to ask for it, then talking to your boss is probably the right thing to do.

Fear should not control your life. It should guide you on the things that you should put all your willpower on. A salesperson that is afraid of making sales calls should start making sales calls right after they arrives at the office. A student who is afraid to write their book review assignment should open their computer right now and start writing. If your office is a mess and you know you have to clean it but you haven't got around to it, then you are afraid of something. You need to identify that fear that leads you to procrastinate and attack it head-on.

Whatever your fear is, it becomes less powerful if you prevent yourself from thinking about it too much and start taking the right actions to overcome it. You should face your fears as soon as you identify them. However, you will have a better chance of overcoming them when your willpower is at its peak. This is when our enthusiasm to reach a goal is strongest and we feel we are ready to face anything. This is the kind of elation that we feel when we read something that makes us want to work for our goals or when we hear a speech that makes us want to start working. You should take advantage of this period of great enthusiasm and face your fears.

Many materials induce these types of increased enthusiasm. You could listen to upbeat songs with messages that you can relate to. You could also listen to motivational speakers. You should choose the materials that best fit your interests. However, you need to remember that these materials only bring out the energy and mindset to reach your goals. Most of the time, we already know the message of these materials. We just need to be reminded of them constantly. This will be discussed more in a later part of this book.

Remove overthinking out of the equation

We spent the previous parts of this book in creating a detailed action plan that will help you reach your goals. We also discussed how you can create schedules that will prioritize the completion of your goals. Now that you know what tasks to do and when to do them, you should make sure that you do each task and not procrastinate from doing them. Fear will make you procrastinate. It will make you overthink the possible bad outcomes.

In worst cases, your mind will even justify not doing the tasks. The best remedy against this is to stick to the actions that you need to do and start doing them. If your schedule tells you that you need to write a 1000-word essay, then you should have nothing in your mind but the word "write". In similar fashion, if your schedule tells you that you need to talk to your boss, you should have nothing on your mind but the phrase "talk to my boss."

This technique is similar to the use of a mantra by people who meditate. When they meditate and they want to shape their mindset, they try to repeat a certain word or phrase over and over. This helps them to attain the state of mind that they want to get to.

By clearing your mind of all the other distractions other than your goals, you will be able to make it focus and prevent other thoughts from influencing your actions.

Chapter 3 Week 2: Clear Internal And External Clutter

There are two types of mess that you need to deal with if you want to become organized: internal and external mess. We need to take care of these two types of mess to be able to move on and start reaching for our goals.

Internal Mess

Internal mess is the constant barrage of thoughts that occupy your mind. Our attention is limited by these constant thoughts. If we keep on entertaining all these thoughts, then we will never be able to keep our attention focused on our goals.

External Mess

People who can't take care of the mess in their minds start to show it in their behavior and their habits. One of the most obvious manifestations of this is a messy living space and workplace. Each of us has the tendency to fall behind in the task of cleaning and organizing our homes. You really need help in organizing your life if your home or office spaces are always messy and the mess is affecting your productivity.

What to do?

Many gurus will tell you to deal with the internal mess first and the external mess will follow. Clearing the thought clutter in your mind however is a continuous process. To help speed up the process, you can start clearing out your external mess first.

You can start by organizing the things in the places where you spend most time. This may include your office or your cubicle. It should also include your car, as well as your bedroom. Cleaning up these places is usually considered by most as unimportant and not urgent tasks. If you want to make sure that all your living and working spaces are organized, then you should move them up to "important but not urgent" tasks.

Though the task of cleaning and organizing does not have a deadline and they could be rescheduled, they should be done regularly if you want to increase your efficiency in working for your goals. There are some areas where you should be the one to organize, like your office. If you can delegate a cleaning responsibility, then consider passing it to someone else.

When organizing everything, you should have functionality as your first priority. If you already have an office system, you could base your office arrangement on this system. If you do not have one yet, then you can use the system that we are about to discuss:

There are three main parts that you need to consider when organizing your office: storage, working space and in/out bins. These are only the basics. You can add other parts if you want, but these three are the most essential.

Storage

If you want to have a more organized workspace, then you should have a logical way of storing files. When you are done organizing your files, any person should be able to find the things that they need to find in your filing system. When filing, make sure to store documents with similar functions together. For example, financial reports should be grouped together in the same container while client contracts should be grouped in another container.

When you have grouped all files by functions, you should also have a sorting system in the inner level. In this case, your judgment is required to pick the right sorting system. For instance, a file for storing clients' contracts could be sorted using alphabetical order, while files about financial reports should be sorted using chronological order.

Do the same with your computer. Label all folders according to the nature of the files found in them. The files in them should also be labeled and sorted using the alphabetical order or by date.

Working space

Organizing your workspace will also help you organize your mind when working. It is important to compartmentalize a certain space for only one type of work. For instance, if your business requires you to call people often, then you can have a cubicle specially designed for that purpose. If you work on the computer all day, for instance, then make sure that the computer where you work does not have games or other distracting apps that can take away your attention from the task that you should be doing.

There are some workspaces however that are multipurpose, like an office table. If you have such a workspace, then you should make sure to organize it to allow you to work on any project instantly without any major preparations. That means that you need to have a wide enough space for the usual types of work that you need to get done. On your office table for example, you should keep the center part free when the table is not in use. That space will become occupied when you work.

However, every time you are done working, make sure to clean up and keep the workspace free. Try to take the minimalist approach when designing your office table. The design should not be distracting. If possible, clear the top of the table of things that are not often used. For instance, you could remove all the redundant office supplies on top of the table and place them inside one of the desks. You should also try to minimize the wires that come from all your communication and electrical devices. Cords and wires that are often used should be labeled. Labeling them will save you time each day by avoiding the need to sort out bundles of wires.

On the computer screen, your workspace is usually your desktop view. You should try to remove all the clutter from the desktop view to prevent distractions from influencing your actions. If you are not using them for business for instance, then shortcuts to social networks should not be visible in your computer desktop view. Put only the most important and most commonly used files in this view.

In and out bins

You should also include two important bins for sorting out work that needs to be done. Each day, you should sort out your "In basket" and make sure that important and urgent tasks get prioritized. If you have an assistant to assist you, then create a system for when files should be removed from the "out basket."

Your Living Space

An organized living space will also help you keep your mind organized. If you arrive to a clean and organized home after a day of hard work, then you will have a better disposition while resting.

If your current living space is too disorganized, you should include cleaning and organizing in your list of tasks. Place it under the "important but not urgent" tasks.

If you have to clean up your whole house, then you should start with the places where you spend most of your time. For most people, this includes the bedroom, bathroom and kitchen. When organizing your environment, you are trying to develop a system that will make moving in a specific space efficient. When organizing your bedroom for example, you should consider the function of the room. Bedrooms are meant for resting. With that in mind, minimize the amount of clutter in the room that's not related to resting. All the stuff that needs to be stored in the room should be hidden from sight.

If possible, place all the things related to work in another room. If you do not have a home office, you can use a simple divider to create one within your bedroom. The stuff that is related to work should be kept in the office side of the room. These things should not end up on your bed.

When organizing your kitchen and your bathroom, you should have their function at the top of your mind. They should allow easy and fast movements. That means there should be enough space to maneuver quickly. There may be some instances when you will need to grab a quick snack for the road. If this is the case, then you should have an organized way to store your snacks. You could hang a shoe organizer on one of the walls and fill it with ready to eat snacks that you can just grab when you are about to leave. In the case of kitchens, you need to set a schedule for when you will replenish your supplies.

The same principles apply when organizing your bathroom. Your mind will be clear if you minimize the amount of stuff visible in your bathroom. You need to be creative when trying to hide the clutter in your bathroom. For instance, you could use a hinged painting to cover unwanted marks on the wall. Instead of putting your toothbrushes on top of the sink, you could store them inside your medicine cabinet. You can also be creative when storing your towels.

Getting rid of stuff you don't need

You should also accept that you own some things that you no longer need. This is true for both appliances and clothes. Organized people do not hoard. If you want to minimize the amount of work when organizing your stuff in the future, then get rid of some of your unused stuff.

You should start with the stuff in your bedroom. The bedroom is where we often store things that we intend to use in the future, but never actually do. You could start with your wardrobe and shoes. Organize your shoes and clothes according to when you last used them. The things that you use every day should be stored separately from clothes and shoes that have not been used for 6 months. If you have not used something for a year, you should consider getting rid of it.

You could get rid of your stuff by giving them away to people you know or to charity. If you are feeling a bit entrepreneurial, then you can also sell some of your things that are still useful. With the help of the Internet, getting rid of your things through selling has never been easier. You could do this every January for example, so that people will be expecting it. You can use social media to announce your sale to your friends.

Chapter 4: Week 3: Defending Your Mind From Clutter

Now that you have organized your environment, it is time to actively keep your mind organized. As for your mind, you need to develop certain habits that will keep it in top shape to reach your goals. In this chapter, we will discuss a collection of skills that will help you keep your mind organized even when you are tired or when you are in a stressful situation.

The power of breathing

Active breathing is one of the most important skills for you to learn if you want to keep your mind at top form for reaching your goals. When you breathe actively, you think and imagine each breath that enters your body. We are so used to passive breathing that we are barely aware that we are doing it most of the time. We need to keep our awareness of breathing because it is one of the most important indicators of our body's current state. When we are feeling extreme emotions for example, we will know about its intensity based on how fast we are breathing. We can say that one of the most obvious physical manifestations of our emotional state is our breathing.

Aside from emotions, breathing also helps us assess our current state of mind. A restless mind is usually accompanied with fast and shallow breathing. This indicates that your mind is not focused and something is distracting it from what you should be focusing on right now.

Breathing not only helps us identify the intensity of our emotions, but it is also our key to controlling them. You can keep your mind organized and goal-centric if you can control your emotions.

How to use your breathing

Just like any skill, you need to practice active breathing regularly if you want to be able to use it at will when it is necessary. You can add this to one of your "important but not urgent activities."

At the same time every day, go to a place where there is not a lot of noise and there are few distracting objects to distract you visually. The place should also be comfortable, because you will need to spend some time in it. You could do this exercise in your room if you do not have anywhere else to go. If there is too much noise in your home, then you can schedule this activity at times of the day when most people are inactive.

For this activity, all you need is a chair to sit on. If you are flexible enough, then you can also sit on a mat and pillow on the floor and assume the lotus position. This is a meditative position used by Buddhists when doing their regular breathing exercises. Other variations of this position are also available for those who are less flexible. However, if you are not comfortable with these floor-sitting positions, then you can just use a regular chair.

Sit on the chair in your chosen location at the same time every day. When doing this activity, you should separate yourself from any distractions. As you sit in the chair or on the floor, you should start breathing normally. You should make sure however, that your back is straight and your tummy is tucked in. Your eyes should also be looking straight at the space 3 feet ahead of you.

As you breathe normally, keep your focus on each breath. Visualize the air coming in and out of your nostrils. You should then count your breaths. This will help develop your ability to focus on even the most menial activities.

Keep a journal

Your mind is an amazing organ. It allows us to think of wonderful ideas that make our lives and the lives of people around us better. We will be able to use it better however if we are aware of how it works and what goes on inside it. By keeping a journal, we are recording our state of mind at a period of time.

When starting a journal writing habit, you should make sure to choose a journal that looks good. Reading journal entries is a lot more enjoyable if you are reading it from high quality paper or a fancy looking notebook. After choosing your notebook, you should then choose a spot in your schedule where you could squeeze this activity in. All you need is around 15-30 minutes every day. It also helps develop the habit faster if you write your journal entry in the same place every day.

Modern day journals

If you prefer to make use of gadgets instead of pen and paper, then you can also start your own digital journal. You can use a Word document to write your journal and save the file as a PDF. You can also create an audio journal. All you need is a sound recorder and enough digital memory to store your files. This is easy to do because all smart phones have recorders nowadays.

If you prefer to take video clips of yourself, then you can also record your journal entries. You will have a more enjoyable time going back to your journal entries if they are videos.

When storing your digital journal entries, you should make sure that you place the date in the file name. You can also include the theme of the journal entry. Lastly, back up your journal files to make sure you will never lose them. You can also use Internet storage services like Google drive or Dropbox to be able to access them anywhere.

Balance your work and exercise

Rest is important in keeping our mind organized. On average, we need to sleep for 7-8 hours every day. As you grow older, the prescribed amount of sleep decreases. Before starting a new sleeping pattern or decreasing your sleeping duration, you should take note of how it affects your productivity.

The best way to manage your sleep is to sleep at the same time every day. There are some occupations that do not support regular sleeping times. If this is the case for your job, then you can try polyphasic sleeping patterns. In these patterns, a person tries to minimize the amount of sleep by taking regular naps all throughout the day.

In addition, you should also do regular workouts to maintain maximum circulation. The mind is also dependent on the amount of oxygen through the blood that it receives. If you exercise regularly, then your circulation will improve and will lead to better oxygenation of the brain.

Take a break from the grind

After a long campaign of going after your goals, there will come a time when short rests are no longer enough. When this time comes, you may need to take a vacation to give your big brain time to rest from the constant stress that you are facing. Many people think that vacations are luxuries for people who have the time and the money. A person can actually improve his productivity when he takes a break to recuperate from stress. Getting your mind off work once or twice a year will help keep it organized. Think of it like a server maintenance downtime for your brain. You will feel fully recharged when you get back to work.

Minimize multitasking

Your brain tries to keep up with the many types of activities that it needs to deal with by creating habits. People who multitask excessively tend to create the habit of multitasking. If they do not actively keep track of their attention span, then the habit of multitasking will cause it to decrease. If done for long periods of time, the attention span of a person may seriously decrease and this may affect the ability of that person to learn new things.

If you want to keep your mind focused for reaching your goals, then you need to make sure that you only multitask menial activities that can be done automatically. Tasks like washing the dishes can be multitasked. Reading a book on the other hand, should be done with one hundred percent focus.

Chapter 5 Week 4: Keeping Yourself Organized

Organizing your life is not a one-time project. In the beginning, it requires constant hard work to get things in order. As mentioned in the previous chapters, you need to take control of the things happening in your environment as well as the thoughts that go through your mind.

After you have done the initial work to organize yourself, you need still to apply continuous effort to keep things organized. This is the process of maintaining the system that you have created.

The Power of Discipline

To continuously have the will to keep things in order, you need to have discipline. This is the most important quality that all successful people have in common. Fortunately, there are a number of things that we can do to help us develop the habit of discipline.

Before we can discuss that, let us first define discipline as it is used in this book. Discipline is a person's ability to do what they need to do at the right time. All the tasks that you scheduled in chapter 1 will all be worthless if you fail to do any of them on time. If you have something that needs to be done at 5 in the morning, then you need to get up, because you are committed to doing that task. If you fail to do that task, then your whole schedule will be ruined because you will need to move every other engagement a few hours later. What if there are some tasks that cannot be moved?

People who lack the discipline to follow their schedules and to keep things organized usually have to redo their schedules in the middle of the week. When they have less time to work with, they tend to let go of some of the important, but not urgent tasks. Lack of discipline will lessen your chances of reaching your goals.

The worst part about lacking discipline is it can become a habit. When you continuously act without discipline, you become accustomed to changing schedules and working in an unorganized environment. This will lead to acceptance of not working at your best and the mediocre results of your work.

People who are more disciplined prefer to work hard at the right time even if they have to sacrifice comfort and immediate gratification. They think ahead and they know that acting with discipline consistently will help them achieve their long-term goals. People who lack self-discipline, on the other hand, prefer to think and even focus on the things that they will achieve now. They are not focused on their long-term goals. They would rather prefer to get sufficient amount of rest and enough coffee before they start working.

Developing self-discipline

Step 1: Control your motivation

To make self-discipline a habit, you must keep your eyes on the prize. By reminding yourself of the things that you are working for, you will be able to push yourself to work even when you do not feel like doing so.

There are two types of motivation: intrinsic and extrinsic motivation. You want to use both of them to generate the necessary drive that will be needed for the long haul.

Extrinsic motivation can be easily created. You need objects from your environment that will remind you of your values and the things that motivate you. A picture of material things that you want to buy, for example, will help motivate you to work harder at your job and get a new promotion.

Though this type of motivation is easy to create, its effects are not permanent. They will sustain your enthusiasm towards work only for a short period of time. Your motivation will probably be gone the next morning.

To make use of extrinsic motivation, you could post photos of the things that you are working for in your workplace. Your motivation will even become stronger if you use pictures of items that you can obtain soon. The sooner the reward, the stronger the motivation that reward creates.

You can also make use of auditory materials like audio books, speeches and even music. All these materials may contain messages that will lift your spirit and help motivate you.

You can make the effects of extrinsic motivation even stronger by using multiple senses to observe what you want. If you want to buy a new car for example, then you can visit a car dealership that showcases the specific model that you want. You could check out the car up close and feel its exterior with your hands. If the salesperson offers you to take it for a test drive, then you can do that. As you enter the car, suck in all that new-car smell. When you drive it, take note of how comfortable the chair is and how smooth the engine goes.

Every time you feel like not working, try to remember the experience of driving the car you want. You can also imagine that car in your driveway. After imagining it, you should go back to reality and convince yourself to get back to work.

Extrinsic motivation will help you create enthusiasm towards work instantly. If you want a more permanent source of motivation however, then you need to develop intrinsic motivation. This type of motivation is derived from your deepest beliefs, values and principles. These types of thoughts are the reason why you push yourself to do things. If your motivation is derived from them, then you will be able to motivate yourself at will, without the need for extrinsic objects and motivational materials.

Keep your eyes on the prize

The best way to increase your extrinsic motivation is by developing a system that will remind you of the tangible things that you are working for. Some people re-motivate themselves every day by writing down their goals daily. This allows them to review their commitments and the methods that they use to reach these goals. Others use the same time every day to view their vision board. This is a corkboard where they post photos of the things that they want to have.

How to develop intrinsic motivation

Prevent self-sabotaging thoughts

Self-sabotaging thoughts can be in many forms. They could be in the form of excuses. Making reasons to justify why you can't do something is a common tactic used by undisciplined people. They are using logic to make themselves believe that failing is okay.

Self-sabotage could also be in the form of self-pity. Thinking that you are not good enough starts as a result of low self esteem. However, when used as a habitual excuse, self-pity can also cause you to lose motivation. Most of the time, no amount of extrinsic motivation can help you if you have these types of thoughts.

Believe in yourself

If you are able to vanquish your self-sabotaging thoughts, then you will be able to make yourself believe that you have the necessary skills, intelligence and talent to reach your goals. Saying "I can do it!" to yourself right before a big task will significantly improve your motivation. One of the best ways for you to constantly convince yourself that you are fit to do a task is by constantly gaining personal victories. You can do this by fulfilling the commitments that you make.

If you promise yourself that you will wake up 5 in the morning and you are able to do it, pat yourself in the back and consider that as a personal victory. If you look back in your past experiences, you should remember some personal victories that you can use to motivate yourself. For instance, if you aced a difficult exam in college, you could try to remember all the hard work that you went through to get the favorable outcome that you wanted. By reminding yourself of personal victories, you will be able to convince yourself that hard work truly does pay off.

Controlling your emotions and thoughts

Now that all the self-sabotaging negative thoughts are gone and you have replaced them with positive motivating thoughts, you should make sure that you control your mind to prevent unwanted thoughts from entering. People who are used to being disciplined can compartmentalize their thoughts and only think of the tasks at hand when they are at work. For people who are beginners at being disciplined and organized, this is easier said than done. However, it can be learned through constant practice.

We often fail to compartmentalize when strong emotions set in when we are working. Emotional people fail to continue their work when they are in a strong emotional state. For undisciplined people, strong emotions can often become an easy excuse to use when avoiding difficult tasks. If you want to keep your mind and environment organized, then you should try to assess your emotions effectively and try to prevent them from affecting other areas of your life.

Creating a commitment with other people

If you are working with other people on a specific task, then it is easier to force yourself to get on with a task. It is hard to let go of tasks in your schedule when other people are depending on you. Collaboration is a great way to motivate you and start a habit of self-discipline. If this strategy works for you, you should use it in the early parts of your week to establish a personal victory early on.

Identify what makes you tick

By that, I mean the things that really motivate you to do the things you do. For instance, though many salespeople are motivated by the commission, there are some who actually do what they think is best for their customers and clients. To identify these factors within you, you should learn about the principles that you abide by and the ones that you want to incorporate in your character.

Your moral and mental traits create your character. They are unique to you and are guided by principles that you have passively or actively included in your character. Principles are the laws of your mind. For you, the principles that you abide by are the truth. The collections of principles that you already abide by are the basis for how you act. Normal people are not aware of the principles on which their behaviors are based. By learning about the principles that influence your behavior, you will be able to actively change them and add more principles to your character.

If you have the principle of excellence for example, then you will not allow yourself to produce a subpar quality of work. People who abide by the principle of punctuality, for instance, are not comfortable with being late to an event or at passing requirements. These are only two examples of principles that will motivate you to become more disciplined.

You should try to examine what principles are already embedded deep into your character and try to make use of them. By being aware of these principles, it will be easier for you to know what good qualities you have that will help you achieve your personal goals. You may also find out through self-examination that there are other principles that you should start to integrate into your daily practices.

Step 2: Stick with your schedule

Doing tasks at the time set for them is also a practice of self-discipline. When doing the tasks you did in chapter 1, you should make sure that you do all the things at the time assigned to them. Even when you finished one task early, you should not move on to the next scheduled task. Wait for the time stated on the schedule before starting the next task.

Schedules allow us to become more disciplined by making us prioritize goals and arrange activities according to those priorities. By sticking to the right time for doing things, you will practice the feeling of constraint and practice your ability to wait. Discipline requires that you do a task at the right time, not early or late.

Step 3: Accept your weaknesses and work around it

Many people try to force themselves into doing things. This will only work if you already have a habit of exercising pure will to get things done. Most beginners, however, do not have enough willpower to go against old habits. A heavy sleeper for instance, will find it very difficult to wake up 3 hours earlier than usual. If you have this problem and you are forcing yourself to wake up 3 hours early, then you will fail miserably because your body is not ready for the commitment that you are trying to stick to.

If you want to accomplish the task of waking up 3 hours early, then you need to accept the fact that your mind is still weak when dealing with drowsiness. You need to work around the goal rather than just forcing yourself to achieve it. Because you know you can't wake up that early, you should arrange your schedule so that you go to sleep 2 to 3 hours earlier the night before. You could also plan the things that you do after you wake up and memorize them so that you don't wake up not knowing what to do.

You could also change the alarm music in your clock to increase the likelihood that you will wake up when it sounds. These are only some of the strategies that you can use to improve your chances of reaching the goal. However, you can only get these things done if you first acknowledge your weakness. Only when you accept your weaknesses can you develop the strategies needed to reach your goals.

When we talk about weaknesses, we should also include temptations that are too difficult to resist for you. Each of us has different weaknesses when it comes to temptations. A chain smoker for instance, will have a difficult time quitting if they do not take any special measures to do so. If the smoker wants to quit, then they should change their lifestyle so that they avoid all the other people surrounding them who also smoke.

Most people set their goals without being fully aware of the necessary steps that they should take to accomplish them. In our smoker example, there may be a need for the smoker to get rid of all the things that theu own that are associated to smoking. They may also limit their meetings with friends who smoke and arrange their schedule to remove all smoking breaks. By removing all the temptations, the smoker has a higher chance of success in quitting.

Step 4: Toughen up against emotional distress

Changing your life to reach a goal is not easy. It will take a lot of willpower to get your act together. There will be some instances when you will feel discomfort or stress when you are doing something new. You should be accustomed to this feeling of stress and discomfort.

If you want mediocrity, then you should design your lifestyle to avoid all sources of stress. On the other hand, if you want to achieve great things, you need to accept that stress exists and you need a way to manage it. In the beginning, you may need some helpful techniques that will minimize the effects of stress on you and allow you to focus on your goals.

As you chase more challenges, you will become accustomed to the stress that each type of challenge presents. Exposing your mind to stress helps establish the premise that you can handle it. By having successful experiences of dealing with stress, you are creating more precedents that you can use as sources of motivation later on.

If you are the type of person who has been avoiding stress all your life however, you need to slowly increase the degree and duration of stress that you face. Making an abrupt increase in your stress levels may overwhelm you. Our goal is to manage stress and not burn you out.

Chapter 6: After The One-Month Challenge: Dealing With Shortcomings

At the end of the 4th week, you should already have some idea of the amount of progress that you have made. If you continued your time tracking up to this point, you should have enough data to assess your actions for the last month.

In this chapter, we will discuss how you deal with failure. It is important to remember that there is only true failure when you quit. Not reaching your goals is not a failure, it is merely a sign that you are not using the right strategy or you are not taking the right amount of action.

It is possible that you reached all the goals that you stated at the beginning of the month. Realistically however, there are some of us who missed our goals. Most people will resort to self-pity and other types of self-sabotaging thoughts. If you let these things rule your mind, then your thoughts will become disorganized again. A disorganized mind will soon manifest in a person's surroundings. If they do not take control soon, then all the progress that they made in the One-Month Challenge will be gone and they will be back to square one.

Follow up failure with action

You should not give up even if you did not hit your mark. All you have to do is to assess the data from your time tracking and compare it with your scheduled tasks. Were you able to stick to all your tasks? Which tasks did you constantly miss? Your goal in assessing your actions for the past month is to identify the reason behind why you failed to reach your goal.

When probing the reasons behind your actions in your time tracking data, you should identify the factors that motivated the actions and inactions that led to failure. Look into reasons why you missed waking up on time or failed to start a task. If you procrastinated, then acknowledge that the reason behind your procrastination is fear. You should identify that fear to be able to deal with it.

For instance, many perfectionists are habitual procrastinators. Many of them are afraid to start a task because they are afraid to start something that they cannot finish perfectly. This is why they keep on procrastinating when it should be time to work.

Once the reasons behind the failure are clear to you, you should try to develop the right strategies to deal with your shortcomings. You should go back to the tips and strategies discussed in this book to help you with that.

Conclusion

Thank you again for downloading this book!

I hope this book was able to help you to organize your whole life.

The next step is to use the tips and strategies in this book to reach for your other goals. You should also continue to work for the goals that we set in this book. The more goals you reach, the more confident you will become. If you fail to reach a goal, don't give up. You should be relentless and tenacious when reaching for the goals that you want.

After you reach the goals that you want, look for more goals and continue to improve. Only through constant practice can you keep your life organized and productive.

Thank you and good luck!

www.ingramcontent.com/pod-product-compliance
Lightning Source LLC
Chambersburg PA
CBHW070843310526
45793CB00011B/522